Skinny Eighth Avenue

4/27/07 NYC
for Kathleen (not Billy, not Mary!) Martin—
the exquisite and sere of music of the Midwest in Manhattan.
Yours,
Stephen Paul Miller

Skinny Eighth Avenue

Poems by **Stephen Paul Miller**

ILLUSTRATED BY NOAH MAVAEL MILLER

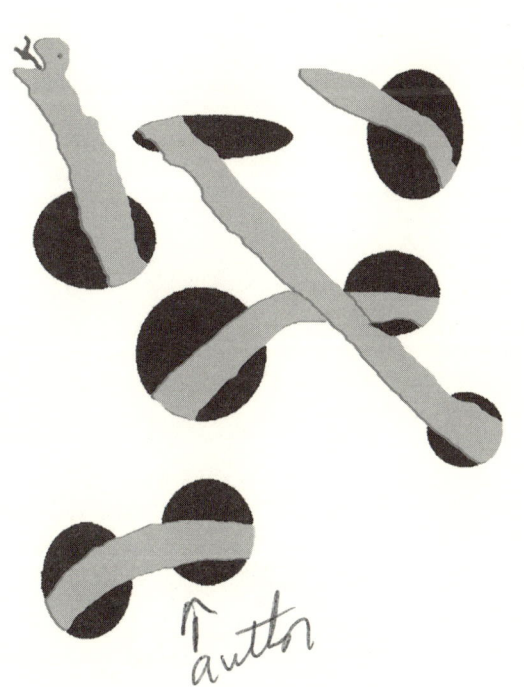

↑author

MARSH HAWK PRESS
EAST ROCKAWAY, NEW YORK
2005

Copyright © 2005 by Stephen Paul Miller

All rights reserved.
No part of this book may be reproduced in any form or by any means, electronic or mechanical, including printing, photocopying, recording, or by any information storage or retrieval system, without permission in writing from the publisher.

05 06 7 6 5 4 3 2 1 FIRST EDITION

Marsh Hawk Press books are published by Poetry Mailing List, Inc., a not-for-profit corporation under section 501 © 3 United States Internal Revenue Code.

Printed in the United States of America by McNaughton & Gunn.

Photos: David McIntyre
Book and cover design: Claudia Carlson
The text of this book is Adobe Garamond with Eras for display.

LIBRARY OF CONGRESS CATALOGING-IN-PUBLICATION DATA

Miller, Stephen Paul, 1951–
Skinny Eighth Avenue / Stephen Paul Miller.— 1st ed.
    p. cm.
ISBN 0-9759197-1-7
1. National characteristics, American—Poetry.
2. Jews—Poetry. 3.
Jewish poetry. I. Title.
PS3613.I553S58 2005
811'.54—dc22

MARSH HAWK PRESS
P.O. Box 206
East Rockaway, New York 11518-0206
www.marshhawkpress.org

for Noah's cousins

Contents

1. STAR TURN

*I'm Trying to Get My Phony Baloney
Ideas about Metamodernism into a Poem*   3
Star Turn   18
Pleasure   21

2. LIVING WITH YOU IS A COMMUNITY

On the Plane   33
George Whatever Bush. or It's in the Bagh, Dad   34
Living with You Is a Community   39
Iraq Iran the Clock   43
You Think Your Dream Is Real Because You Can't Feel the Bed   44

3. OVERFLOWING POCKETS

Officer Stephen Paul Miller   51
Cybersqualor   53
Marilyn, as an Actress in a Play, Starts It   55
Overflowing Pockets   56

4. HUSTLING

Skinny Eighth Avenue   63
*"The Hustle" and Its Liquid Totems
of Holocaust, Suburb, and Computer*   65

5. PHOTO POSTS

Photo Post   75
All Visual Materials Emit Countless Cartoon Bubbles   76

6. DEVIL'S WAX

George W. Burning Bush   83
Devils' Wax   84
Potato Chip   85

Acknowledgements   86
About Author and Illustrator   87

LIST OF ILLUSTRATIONS BY NOAH MAVAEL MILLER

1. Cover and page iii, "Skinny Eighth Avenue"
2. "Hands," page 1
3. "Shirts," page 4
4. "Brown Mammoth," page 15
5. "Dinosaur," page 19
6. "Buttons," page 31
7. "Cowboy," page 36
8. "Dinosaur Skeleton," page 37
9. "Yo-Yo," page 45
10. "No More Bad Presidents," page 47
11. "Jump Bunny," page 51
12. "Woolly Mammoth 6000," page 55
13. "Gray Elephant," page 59
14. "Turtle," page 61
15. "Skinny Eighth Avenue 2," page 64
16. "River Line," page 71
17. "Dream Horse," page 73
18. "Mosasaur," page 75
19. "ELEPhant," page 79
20. "Cutty," page 81
21. "Peace with a Woolly Mammoth," page 85

1. Star Turn

I'm Trying to Get
My Phony Baloney Ideas about
Metamodernism into a Poem

I forget
    our SeaWorld
        discounts.
           "We save
                30 or 40 dollars."
                    "So what?"
                      objects
                          my 7-yr.-old son
                  Noah.
                "Money's
                a stupid little man
              who makes you
          buy things."
        Post-17th century
    modernism
pushes what follows
          like a vacuum cleaner
                salesman
                    selling
                  one
              more part,
        says Bruno Latour.
      As we turn
    Noah calls
  the highway,
set like
  a thin
    valley in a wide
      South Californian hill,
            "a lowway."
              We run into a new
                    doctors'
              convention
        at the Delmar Hilton,
    and I enjoy coffee in a china cup
  "Can there be
    an invention convention?" asks Noah from
the back seat on the way to SeaWorld.
Greeks say "postmodern"
    to describe
      a style

after one
        "of the moment,"
                —as modern means—
                          but now
                   the postmodern
            follows
       World War II,
so say "post-World War II/modernism."
              Thank you!!!
                     World War II
         globalizes America.
    Postmodernism Americanizes
  the world.
  I'm not
so much
American as
    similar to it.
       That's bull.
          Noah sees me writing and says
             "anything you say can be a poem."
        Example?
Near three SeaWorld sprinklers
     he reads Shamu the Whale's
        cartoon bubble: "Caution, Wet Area."
In the bathroom Shamu says:
     "Caution, Wet Floor."
       "Shamu really cares if
people slip," laughs Noah. We go back to the sprinklers
                  and soak
     though you never know
   which sprinkler'll squirt.

"We are always naked," says Noah,
　"and have to grow clothes you can't take off not to be."

　　　　Sprinklers are more enjoyable with shirts on.

　　　"Don't throw away any of your old T-shirts—
　　　　　　　　　　　　they might fit me."

　　　　　　　　　　I'm not so much American
　　　　　　　　as similar to it,
　　　　the idea, I mean,
　　the reports
tricking
　　people into coming
　　　　　to North America
　　　　　　in the 1620's
　　　　　　and Iraq in 2003.
　　　　　　　　　　"I don't see why they
　　　　　　　　　　　call it SeaWorld,
　　　　　　　　　　　where's the sea?
　　　　　　　They should call it WaterWorld.
　　　　　　SeaWorld doesn't
sound good. I don't
　　　mean the music.
　　　　　　　I mean
　　　　　　　　the word."
　　　　　　　　　　The sound
　　　　　system plays "Elephants on Parade."
　　　"Whatever happens
　to Dumbo's mother?"
asks Noah, "I forget."
　　"Dumbo gets a good job and uses his
　　　　　　　influence to
　　　　　　　　spring his mom
　　　　　　　　　　from jail."
　　　　　　　"Oh yeah," he recalls,
　　"The stork makes a mistake
　　　　　and delivers
　　　　　　an African elephant
　　　　　　　with big ears
　　　　　　　　to an Asian mother."
　　　　　Like America,
　　I think magically.
　I can send myself letters

· 5 ·

offering infinite
            gifts.
                    So what's the prob?
                            Of course,
                                    Allies won't fight
                                                for Jews—
                            but the Second World War
                    sets a stage
        for Eisenhower
coining
    "Judeo-Christian"
            a few years after he and Patton
                inspect a death camp, making
                    Patton sick. Ike orders his troops
                    to see
                        what they fight against, just
                    as Bob Hope
                        shows them what they fight for
                        in Patty Thomas,
                            a girl the opposite
                                of a concentration camp.
                                        So how can
                                                seemingly hip
                                        people like
                Samantha Power (*Problem
from Hell*)
    say people discover
                the Holocaust in
                        the seventies as
                                if the post-war
                                        concentration
                                camp *Life*
                        photos
                and Nuremberg
    and other shockers
don't register.
            I ask Samantha Power
                        what she means
                                and she explains that it's
                        not until
                    the seventies
and eighties that the Holocaust
                    as a notion "galvanizes" us. Huh?
    Maybe she means the Holocaust's

upshot is hard to quantify until much later. Power concerns
 herself with
 genocide's identification, criminalization,
and prevention, which takes documentation,
 but that's still different
 from using the Holocaust
 as the reason to circle the wagons
and help provide the illusion
 of moral high ground for
 Islamicist mafias.
 This is something to die for,
 a legacy for my great aunts and uncles
 and cousins?
 Relatives help so much on this trip. My nephew
Matt books cheap hotels and rents cars on Priceline.
 That's how I learn it works.
And my cousin Harriet drives us to Redondo Beach where
 we play with her dogs and dolphins leap like
 deer.
 See, the Holocaust brings something soft.
 Maybe.
I can't explain.
As a freed prisoner I might
 starve my former guards, but enough,
 as Brando's Godfather says.
 In America, the Second World War
 crowns the New Deal—
full employment now!
 Reports of FDR
 trying to impress
 his secretary
 indicate he
 looks forward
 to spending
 on peace
 as he does on war,
 GI bill-like programs
 forever the norm.
I think the Reagan
 Revolution
 begins when so few
 support
 New Deal-style
 employment progams

        during economic slumps
of the mid- and late seventies.
                      (Note no ex-governor becomes
president between FDR and Jimmy Carter—Truman,
                                    Eisenhower,
          Kennedy, Johnson, Ford come from
        national and international bodies:
   Senate, House, 'n
Command of Allied Forces.) But,
       after Nixon, the final
    budget and economic
           solution
               is cutting social
                   spending,
   that mind-set prevailing under Ford
  and Carter.
The Democrats
    fall
       when no one
          pushes.
              What happens?
                  On the hotel TV,
        Bullwinkle J. Moose as
     Mr. Know It All
shows a vacuum "customee"
how to sell vacuums
by sticking his foot in a prospective "custo-mower"'s door
                     and then
        SpongeBob and Patrick sell
    chocolate
  door to door,
buying chocolate bags
    from the fish
      at the first house they visit
             and bags for those bags
     from the same fish
   at the next house.
That's what happens.
   Whenever we try to sell we buy.
          Seventies Democrats sell so little.
  The New Deal, Arthur Schlesinger calls it
Jeffersonian ends
 thru Hamiltonian means,
  morphs to post-war

spending
　on human capital and highways
　　providing new
　　　suburban privileges
　　　　for the middle class
　　　　　(suburbs are previously much more high end)
　　　　　　but stigmatizing the poor and
　　　　　　　in a sense shedding parts
　　　　　　　　of the whole
　　　　　　　　　the ND represents,
　　　　　　　　　　as if some hegemonic collective sense
　　　　　　　　　　　of America tries to rebalance itself,
　　　　　　　　　　　　eat the same piece of cake again,
　　　　　　　　　　　　　deconstruct out of spite.
　　　　　　　　　　"We've been
　　　　　　　　　　　　in California so long
　　　　　　　　　　　　　　it seems
　　　　　　　　　　　　　　　like Manhattan,"
　　　　Noah says near the end of our stay.
　　　Is America tipping again?
　　We've been after WW II so long it seems like before it.
I sense W'll lose again [can you tell me what happens?] but
　it's nonetheless odd
　　how easily
　　　white folk support him.
　　　　　Rootless mobs implement fascism,
　　　　　　　Arendt's *Origins of Totalitarianism* theorizes.
If America's a big rootless mob
　　anything's possible.
　　　　I said "if."
　　　　　　Suburbanization divides
　　　　　　　　　and conquers, but I don't mean
intentionally, since it sells what people want,
　　a centuries-old fear of the city. Suburbs
　　　　compartmentalize strangers while we
　　　　　　buy more and more land on time
　　　　　　　from someone else
　　　　　　　　who buys even more
　　　　　　　　　　　　land on time.
　　　　　　　　　Maybe the same guy
　　　　　　sells all the time,
　but seemingly everyone can have a castle.
　The New Deal coalition holds
　　till the suburbs that it fashions

become so pervasive there's I suppose less city to exploit,
lowering surburban standards of living so
    suburbs (including third world suburbs) must produce,
   and there seems less
stress on the federal
  government-stuff your congressional representative
                            brings home,
                which seems more from
         the congressperson than the feds.
But the fulcrum tilts when we realize we
     need a real federal government with a real president,
although most can't quite say that's what they want,
                            so they teeter
            on favoring Kerry over Bush.
After all, we only get Roosevelt
             from the post-WWI/Great Depression crisis
      that luckily doesn't
give us Mussolini, Stalin, Hitler,
          Franco, Mao, or others
             arising from that
             historical moment.
                 On the rocks
                  of that crisis,
                    here in La Jolla,
                      I sense Venice '72
           after the Republican convention
          must be moved from San D to Miami
           due to the ITT-S. Diego
           convention bribery
       scandal,
and near Venice beach that August
                I see Republican Convention headlines
        while a young blonde woman with a poncho
      spoon-feeds me
    yogurt
  in a Buick
 facing the beach
and Sammy D.
   sucker-hugs
     our beaming Prez
        although Archie
              Bunker
              won't hug Davis—
              what year did that episode run?

                    On Ocean Beach I meet Risa, a
               seventies friend of a friend,
      now an Atlanta social worker
            vacationing
                 with her family.
                      Risa catches up.
                           "You haven't changed at all: When I think 'Steve
                                 Miller,' I think 'borderline depressed.'"
                           Why are we in California anyway?
                      To me California means
      back to the Garden—
                 but more immediately I'm here
                           to cheer my son.
                                Risa tells me her sister
                                      has what my wife has
                                           and her nephew Ray
                                                 thinks Risa's his mother.
                                      On the highway,
                                           I point at a Red Lobster
                                           and remind Noah
                                                 how Mommy liked
                                                      going there with us.
                                      He doesn't want to remember.
                           To cheer him up,
                      I tell
           the Risa and Ray story.
      As we drive to lunch Eric Clapton's
                 song to his dead son plays.
                      I tell Noah about it
                 to make him feel better
      and it works. Noah criticizes
      Clapton's son's mother as
            we pass an intricate accident
                 shaving off a car's
                      front end. Feeling better,
                           Noah enjoys pancakes at a Denny's
                           where the bathroom door says "MENS."
                                      "It should be 'M-E-N-apostrophe-S'
                                 or 'M-A-N'S.' Hey," Noah speculates,
      "Maybe, this is THE MAN'S bathroom."
      The urinal mat says
      "Say NO to Drugs."
                 "What does the toilet have to do with it?" wonders Noah.
                      "Do they want you to throw your drugs in the toilet?"

· *11* ·

                                        Noah wonders.
I phone my LA friend Ken Deifik who says he forgot
  how articulate
    the people they interview
      in *Woodstock* are until seeing the new director's cut.
Whatever the sixties is it melds
                        natural and
                          human concerns
                            unlike unions of
                                "human" and
                                "natural" science
        resembling Nazi laboratories and Utopias.
The modern is the nature/human split,
  says Latour, and Latour is right:
    "We've never been modern,"
        meaning modernism's always
            an illusion—a dynamic one
                    we can see
                        through
                          but not escape—
            We're meta-, not post-, modern.
        The new contains all.
We're between bad (e.g., Nazi)
  and good (e.g., sixties)
    people/nature distanceless reunions.
                Noah plays in the playground sand
                        near the main La Jolla Beach.
    "Nice warm sand," a kid says.
Ideally, California's public space is everywhere—
                        even if it's really nowhere.
California should be one big Woodstock.
            Okay, I know it's maybe the apotheosis
                            of the suburb,
                the death of public space,
        and the Enlightenment's close,
    since public space enables discourse—
  why suburbs (lacking much publicly owned common
space) and retro Enlightenment Nazis
  can blur. But California can be intimate public space
          where it's easy to have Noah write my poetry,
      I finally see
as *Fahrenheit 911* makes you
                feel,
                    though you thought

                                        you already felt.
                    I should settle for academia not killing me.
Proficide is a crime
               only recently named.
                    A downside of tenure is
                       the scarcity of senior hires,
                         tying profs to one plantation,
                       so employers
                            have a cheap, stable work force
                            and can only fire professors
                         by slowly icing them.
                            The university can be
                            one big
                                 Florida election—overlooking
                                 or lying about evidence,
                                 misinterpreting rules,
                                 stonewalling, not
                                 admitting error
                                 so turning more
                                 and more wrong
                                 until it's
                                     full blown
                                         inhuman torture.
                                         Insensitivity turns
                                         brutal—
                  they might see it in Bush
                     but think they've
                     a solid rationale
                     that just feels right,
                 just as
                 neocons
                 think they
                 don't need
                 to make sense
                 because
                 they're cool.
                 Sometimes
                 I feel that
                 way
                 but it's weird
                 how
               my job
               sort of
        well…misused…

                    well…they put me through
this whole 14th Amendment thing—the way Bush v. Gore
            uses the right to vote to take votes from African-
Americans, again, like *Groundhog Day*,
                you know, because Florida
                        has no uniform way to count votes,
            but then it stops it from
        being corrected
because never mind.
            Similarly,
                the idea is they're not supposed to use
                        past application descriptions,
                            assessments, and judgments
            of research and publications *against you*
so they say
            you can't use past research and publications
                                            at all.
                And then when my wife gets sick,
            the university
                    human resources dept. backs the college
                        of conservative arts and denies
                            me a family leave because they
                                say my wife's too sick
        and needs care outside the home and hence I'm
not caring for her. Huh? It allows them to, as women
                    so often experience, wash their hands
            of harmless special accommodation for dire needs
        and screw up childcare
for the good reason
            of them winning. That's 10% of it.
                    In another poem I'll be more specific, I
        guess, or, oh, forget it.
They're just doing
  what they're supposed to do.
    I shouldn't take it so personal[ly],
      but focus instead on
        eating pizza on the beach with Noah.
                            He asks me what I'm thinking.
                I lie and substitute my last thought: "1968 and
what would have happened?" "Huh?"
                            The sun's
                                setting in the Pacific
                    where Bobby Kennedy dies again.
                How could he get out of Vietnam?

Johnson, McNamara
  et al. already know you can't win and
   they're not stupid.
  But
   losing
    is off the charts.
     To help Noah on a monkey bar
      I take my eyes off the white sun
       and miss the sunset
        yet catch its pink tail.
         We drive off and see Mars and a crescent moon.
                  There're no tall
                  buildings near
               so the
         ocean/light/sun/west
        seem in the same sky
     with the south/moon/Mars/night
  like side-by-side stage sets.
Kissinger says we should have prolonged the Vietnam war
                         indefinitely.
      He says Russians would then
have respected us and not gone into Afghanistan
and presto
     no 9/11! Don't worry,
          though. If the best we can do
            is eternal quagmire
       we
lose one in Vietnam
     to gain one in Iraq.
      Noah whines and I tell him to use his
     words.
    He tells me to use my brains.
  We all want credibility.
The problem is Kissinger wants credibility
      about his being God,
        and Bush can't wait to
     spread good
    government
  when he doesn't believe
in any government.
But Bobby Kennedy can and will end the war.
  We won't dwell on it
    for as long as we actually do—I mean still are.
      Noah and I take a long trip by feeling at home.

When we fly home
we won't go anywhere.
In the morning,
Noah builds a "castle-hole"
from a wall
he makes to protect him from water
when he notes the "hole"
can project upwards.
The kids copying him,
he says,
show they like him.
Four bathers pass.
"That's awesome," says one.
"You raised him well,"
a college-age woman
wearing a bikini tells me
in a Czech accent.
It's lucky I got lost
going to the zoo
and stop
at whatever
this beach is.
One reason for a vacation is to be nowhere.
On the hotel radio
we hear about an "international sand castle contest,"
exciting Noah.
He says he wants to build a castle without being judged,
though, at the very end, he wants to win.
Noah tells the judges,
two thin middle-aged women writing on pads,
his castle has "special features."
He alerts them to the charms
inside the castle: "a path to the roof"
and "a tunnel to a hollow room."
They call all 20 or so (12 and under) kids
onto a stage facing away from the beach
but only acknowledge 3 winners,
leaving the other kids to droop off-stage.
Noah's castle is the only one with formal integrity.
Though three-dimensional and partially hidden,
it's of-a-piece
in terms of its sight lines and psychological space.
"The judges know I won;
they keep their judgments

          on the inside when they should be outside."
     Then Noah clarifies
their apparent
   incompetence:
"They're too serious."
      Noah and I have collaborated
          on a marvelously imperfect meta-vacation
         made of grainy meta-thinking
        and to celebrate
       JetBlue pleasures us
     with snacks,
       no meal of course,
      but supplement,
      nothing but excess.
         Blue feeds you like Social Security—
      it's best not to need it.
       Bring it on,
       they suggest,
        and you can eat
         watching TV.
          There's no movie
           but everyone gets
          a television and
           their house flies.

Star Turn

Esmeralda's for Bush and
    I'm for Esmeralda. I soak in her
                                skin
                              is
                        satin blue
                        piled clear
                          moonlit sky.
        George W. Bush loses the turn
    of Esmeralda's mind.
The Latina vote bounces big, big, big.
You can hear its tinkling army.
Esmeralda smells so good.
I like George W. Bush if Esmeralda
likes her, I mean him.
Esmeralda sneezes.
I like the letters of her name
        reflected off glass—
    the sea from Esmeralda,
  her patterns of sharing.
 Who is the one with Esmeralda?
My son says a wedding's
a wedding because everyone's
so excited they wet themselves.
They're 23% full—
101% electric, not
 like the sixties, but the sixties, love
welcomes an ever-present threat with
   hallucinating muscles that tickle your wizard and distill
    all harm, this is the kind
      of high you feel at home.

       In my beginning is my rear.
     In my rear end
  my beginning. The big snake shines through the smoke
while liberal democracy quivers and Noah thinks,
walking with his ice cream,
"Heaven is the best place on earth."
He's so excited
the apartment jumps into another building and
Esmeralda is at her height.
History's the apocalypse
and no one sleeps.

The big bang addresses itself,
removed of all phony influence.
Esmeralda drinks, then dunks, then slams.
She hoots.
    My head grows high and
enters her stratosphere.
I breathe
       elements
            making love
                   to Esmeralda.

We tumble back in time.
I put on a W.
There is no gravity yet
and light is so smooth.
Esmeralda's hair slopes, smooth
                     as a water slide.
She grows up in Brazilian public housing
and through every facet of her life
        develops the sharpest
and most insightful leadership skills.

Her eyebrows reverberate.

Her ear is a fine marble shell.

She is full professor.

Her crossed arms under her

                    limber breasts,
                        she rises

        as no coffee ever shared.

                She partitions her life into each memoir gene.
            Her wrists are large
    for such a slender woman.
I find harmony in her strong
            round shoulders,
  as she grasps them with her subtly
  scented palms and fingers.
Esmeralda teaches business.
She set up worldwide
  Technology Interchange-
      exchange Network (WTIN).
We need Esmeralda.
Our troops are too stretched.
"It's too cold,"
Noah says,
"to drink soda,
so I'll slurp my pizza."
We already know the answers but
ecstasy fills a bucket as worthy rain
interjects new singularities.

Knowing almost nothing about
   Esmeralda as an average woman of genius,
       the university treats her as a nuisance.
They don't see her rays of know-how even as
    she shapes them.   Her powers bend the past.
She makes us so skinny at the hips as she rises.
Her substance
      and ideas propel me. She wears these
           amazing slacks below
                      her navel and waist.
How does she get her luminously-smooth
lavender-pink pleated silky silk pants
     to accent the tints in her voice?
I'm everyone in my class. I laugh as I sneeze. Our clicks align
   and the distraction
     imbues resonance.
The young stars turn.

This is Esmeralda. (See attachment.)

Pleasure

What is Jewish poetry, or,
                    at least
one kind of Jewish poetry?

Putting aside all-encompassing definitions and
            tautological-"Jewish-poetry-is-as-Jewish-
                        poetry-does"-responses,
                I find myself
                    examining my own experience,
                        asking
                            "What sounds Jewish?"
                or, more to the point,

"What does 'Jewishness' sound like?"

I'm not sure, of course, and thankfully
            there's no simple answer,
    but while driving I entertain
    my 90-year-old ma by
            turning the radio to
                    Steve Somers'
    Yiddish nuanced sports-talk schtick.
                She immediately
identifies him as Jewish and is happy
(though she cares nothing for sports).

        I ask how she
                so quickly
    picks up "Jewishness" in his voice
    and she eventually theorizes

the Yiddish accent comes from dovening,
            the Yiddish word for prayer sharing Indo-
        European roots with "divine."

Dovening as praying doesn't exclude silent prayer,
and my mother knows this, but thinks nonetheless of
                                        dovening
        as rhythmic recitation of Hebrew liturgy
            while rocking back and forth 'n nodding.
        Since dovening is not a Hebrew word,
    in her experience rhythmic dovening

                                        reflects
how Yiddish-and-English-speaking peoples process
                                        Hebrew,
and she sees dovening as an important link between
                            Yiddish and Hebrew,
    noting cadences of dovening in Yiddish.

Okay, I'm not an expert,
  and my mother's theory could be
                    wrong, and even if it's true,
   it might concern only Eastern European Jews.

And yet it might point to something
even further back than Yiddish.

When I think dovening, I think anapest:

unstress-unstress-STRESS

An anapestic rhythm generates, propels us
                                through language
        as dovening does through prayer, and indeed
    ancient Jews
  see time as linear,
            not cyclical
        or restarting with each new king
  but thrusting endlessly from creation
        indefinitely as a
      quite distinctive way of reckoning time,
which I mention to my young son
  on Rosh Hashanah, when I tell him why
   it's 5765. "Do some people still rewind time?" he asks.
And Rosh Hashanah is probably ambiguous
here since the holiday suggests
a movement back to the beginning of creation
to clear space and move forward.

   I won't pretend to know anything about Hebrew—
or even Yiddish—
          or for that matter
      the Aramaic in which Kaddish is chanted,
but I think it's notable that Kaddish

begins in the future tense
anapestically,
constructing motion even
from death:

 yisgadol
yiskadosh—

which are reflexive future
third person singular verbs,
so I think they mean something like:

May He magnify Himself.
May He sanctify Himself.

I'm not sure but the point is it's in the future tense
and so is the word Israel, or Yisrael, meaning something
                                                                 like
he will struggle with God and he will succeed,
suggesting a constantly edgy relation with God.

When I think of a Yiddish accent and the anapest
                                     and a certain Jewish drive, I
think of somehow finding myself chatting
with Jackie Mason on 57th St and 6th Ave.
                      His last words to me are:

"It's a PLEASure to TALK to an <u>inTELL</u>igent PERson."

   I think this sort of anapest lends itself to a
direction indirection surprise!
…direction indirection surprise!
  or
   unstress unstress stress
  ho   hum   wow
  ho   hum   wow
   rhythm. Rhythm is perhaps a better word
than meter here since when performing Jewish
liturgy
      dovening imposes something rhythmic on other
possible metric readings,
       though it could of course be in the meter of
  the text too, and a poem can be enriched by
possibilities of differing meters

       in the same passage,
  maybe a mark between a good poem and
     less good one, between say, "of man's first
disobedience" and "once upon a midnight dreary."
Therefore, I do not mean overly to emphasize the
anapest, or exaggerate its place in the Bible.
The anapest merely indicates, in part through
dovening, tendencies to stress more
generative and dynamic, rather than referentially
reflective,
   poetic
m.o.'s that can accommodate the pace of say
the Marx Brothers' *Duck Soup*
or a Charles Bernstein or David Shapiro poem.
In this regard, the Yiddish accent
might owe
something to both
dovening and
biblical poetry,
perhaps more than Hebrew itself.

Hebrew lives so much through poetry
that dovening and what I'll call
the dynamic and parallel structures
of biblical poetry influence Yiddish,
and other languages Jews use, such as English, AND
Ladino,   Arabic,   Judeo-Persian,
Rumanian,   Judeo-Arabic,
Judeo-Italian, Judeo-Provencal,
Judeo-French, Judeo-Greek,
Judeo-Crimean Tatar, and Jewish Neo-Aramaic—
so it makes sense to clarify that my evidence is very
Eastern-Euro-American, and I think it would be cool if
someone looked into some of these other languages for
biblical poetic influences within their respective
                                      literatures.

Robert Alter finds "the structure of biblical poems is
determined not by any substantive impulse of narration, but
by a steady progression of image or theme, a sort of
mounting semantic pressure which is to say a structure of

                            intensification."
What I say about the anapest

concerns a way to make
   dynamic poesis
       indicating something like
the intensities and
drives
   of biblical poetry as Alter characterizes it
   more than valuing
any particular meter,

       more of a twin phenomenon with
breaking the back of iambic pentameter
then replacing it with another meter,

perhaps relating the new ethnicities
of modern America with modern poetry, and both

perhaps with something "other." Eliot after all says he needs
Paris, a mix of English and not English,
to write "Prufrock."

While vetting this paper with a friend
who probably experiences Judaism much
more directly than me, she says
   Kaddish for her is its trance-like rhythm,
chanting with extremely flat intonation
with a fairly even if at times anapestic delivery.
   For her (Ilana Abramowitz), the meter seems part
of a bigger linguistic dynamic.
Maybe I shouldn't,
   but I think of Eliot's flat rhythmic quality.
In her *21st Century Modernism* book, Marjorie
Perloff talks of
               how
   important Eliot and Pound are in promoting
"generative" and
dynamic poetic models.
Frankly, I haven't been drawn to Eliot and Pound since I
                       was a teenager.
Seeming rigidities and pretensions in their dictions, and
their differing brands of anti-Semitic and fascistic leanings
       make them uncongenial as discursive influences
and yet my teen attraction seems valid.
They are important to what poetry now is.
I find their ambivalence toward

>   Whitman
>   instructive here. Whitman uses the Bible's parallel
>   structures to
>   portray American diversity. I use the plural, "structures,"
>   since there are many different kinds of parallel structures
>   using all manner of syntactic,
>   semantic, and other linguistic constants
>   highlighting changes within a fixed structure.

In a sense, Whitman
remakes modern poetry
in a Jewish tradition,
and renders this influence
unavoidable thereafter.

Certainly Eliot and Pound take parallelism in more
odd, syncopated directions, using different parallelisms and
intensities as the Bible sometimes does. Note "Prufrock"
repeating "let us" to initiate—
"Let us go then, you and I"—
                and respond—
   "Do not ask 'what is it?' Let us go… ."
  And each time Pound's *Canto 45* repeats "with Usura"
it refers to both Usura's previous and following examples.
This kind of dynamic is used in JOB (where, for
example, "do you know?" parallels other "do you"
questions: "Do you know the time when the mountain goat
gives birth,/ do you mark the birth pangs of the gazelles? /
Do you number the months till they come to term? / Do you
know the time when they give birth?" Check out the Bible
and the *Cantos* for more complex interactions among
parallel structures. Similar modes are
available to Pound and Eliot
in poetic devices such as the villanelle and sestina, and in
musical forms, (and the use of these sources in itself
demonstrates a push to the "something else"
of modern poetry) but, in terms of
epic sweeps generating throughout entire poems, Whitman
and biblical poetry cannot be ignored.
             I can't say on what level Eliot and Pound adapt a
                   Jewish model of poetry
              but perhaps it's

            difficult to avoid,
                          especially
      after Whitman unleashes it.
And, obviously being subjective,
Eliot and Pound sometimes seem
  more Jewish than Whitman.
Well, sometimes anyway.
A secular Jewish poet like Kenneth Koch bases
his work in parallel structures *and* a sense of intensity *and* a
                            relentlessly
                ongoing discourse.
By ongoing discourse, I mean talk
flowing to and fro like dovening yet also
hurtling
     seemingly endlessly forward.
Perhaps parallelism, discourse, and intensity
                are related hallmarks of
     something like Jewish poetry. Its parallelisms and
intensities dovetail with argumentative, narrative,
and/or referentially abstract, linguistically
reflexive
poetry that, as Duke Ellington puts it, swings. Ellington,
backstage, wearing a Bowler with sleepwear, once signed
my *Confucian Odes* Pound translation

near where it says "the Duke rings true"
and also close to words to the effect of

"everything comes to the Duke"
(though not exactly those words)

and around 1930 James Weldon Johnson says

  Jews only among white folk can sing
black, and from the Andrews Sisters and Harold Arlen 'n Gershwin
    to Andy Statman, Klezmer and jazz and blues
rhythms and melodies
             easily blend. Lenny Bruce,
living perhaps in a more innocent time,
says black people are, after all, Jewish.
David Antin is Jewish, but Spalding Gray
said he considered himself Jewish too. He might not sound
Jewish though he composes that way through ongoing
discourse. Maybe his neurosis helps.

The generative feature I'm describing might not
dominate all Jewish poetry, but
                    describes some I like.
Perhaps Jewish poetry is concrete and
probing, like the anti-fascism as strong as
fascism that Benjamin tells Brecht he feels taking shape
within him—odd to say when speaking of Eliot and Pound,
but I'm not saying there aren't other workings in both, and
perhaps that's why their obscurities and rigidities
            sometimes seem out of place.

One might expect a healthy dose of skepticism
from Jewish poets Pound influences, and skepticism
preoccupies the poets we
associate with Objectivism,
so many of whom are secular Jews.
Zukovsky and other so-called Objectivists
desire oddly externalized sincerity
virtually embedded in words. Also, suggesting her
preference for the real and sensory, my mother often says
she's from Missouri.
I wish she could vote there.
Objectivism might
have something to do with
what for me is Theodore Herzl's
most compelling reason for a Jewish state—and of course
I'm talkin' a century ago—and for me the
reason the United States at its best might be
a secular Jewish state, that is, a state in which Dreyfus
theoretically gets a fair shake
and the truth a direct presentation.
(The French right never acknowledge
the persuasive case for Dreyfus.
You'd think the truth would be more convincing.
Or at least entertainable.
What am *I* blocking?)
Of course a direct presentation's difficult to achieve, but
the desire's real and sheds light on
how Objectivism paradoxically
involves subjective qualities such as
sincerity when verbally constructed. Note Jerome
Rothenberg's "Poland/1931":
"if there are men who ride the train to lodz/ there are still
jews/ just as there are still oranges/ & jars/ there is still

someone to write the Jewish poem—others to write their
mothers names in light." Norman Finkelstein says
"Poland/1931" is distinctively "Jewish" because it is as
"objective in its identity as a jar or an orange, an
                    utterance...circulating,"
making me think of God promising
Jacob a home as He tells him
                of perpetual Diaspora.
The Jewish imagination is not necessarily
grounded in a nation; Jewish poetry
needn't be by Jews, and Jewish poetic
imagination isn't limited to poetry.
Much of Harold Bloom's fierce rap starts
with the Kabbalah but, in a less overtly Jewish
fashion, the urge to stress language and experience what
makes us see language-as-language as *poetry* is central in
Roman Jakobson's work; knowing cultures as languages is
of course advanced by Claude Lévi-Strauss,
and Derrida makes clear that language is
more than anything else a generative if painstaking "sense
                                      of itself."

That perhaps the preeminent Formalist,
founding "Structuralist," and most philosophically
influential "Post-Structuralist" are secular Jews
    suggests, as secular Jews, they
                          extend a
close attention characteristic of traditional Jewish scholars
                to secular texts that
        magnify
our sense of what texts
can be. Similarly, secular Jewish figures
such as Lenny Bruce and Bob Dylan and, hey, my son just
asks if Simon and Garfunkel are two people, and I don't
know, Rodgers and Hammerstein and Einstein and
Irving Berlin and Lerner and Lowe—okay,
forget Lerner and Lowe, not because they're not Jewish,
no, I like them, and I think they're Jewish—secular Jewish
figures s t r e t c h
linguistic, critical, and poetic substance
        through swinging yet solid dynamically
                            generative spiels.

2. Living With You is a Community

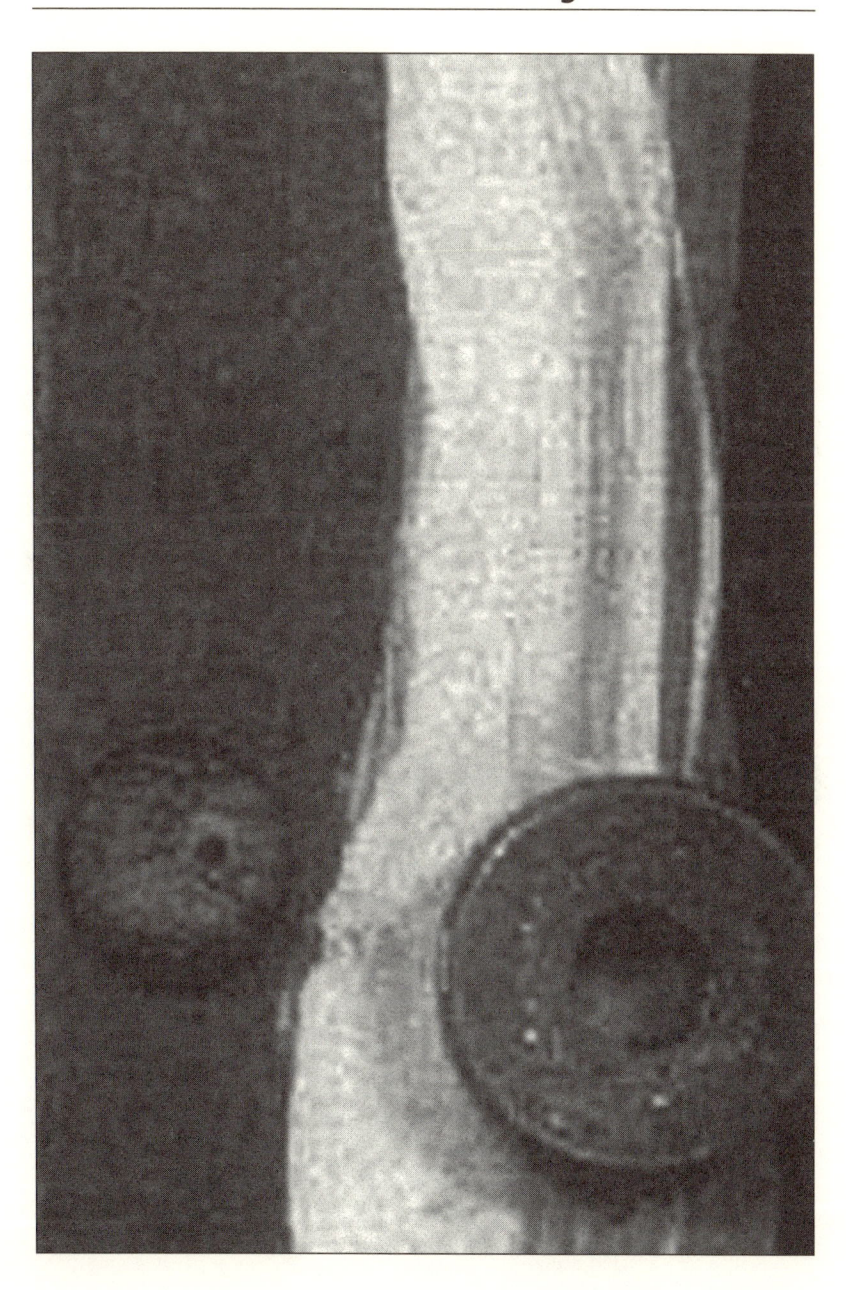

On the Plane

with Anna Kang

Hi, my name is Lick.

Oh.

What's your name?

Shopping.

Can I taste your name?

You can buy it.

Okay, I have 20 bucks in my mouth.
I'd very much like
       to lick your name.

It's 20 plus tax.

SHOPPING TAKES MONEY OUT OF HIS MOUTH.
HE MAKES A LICKING SOUND AS HE SAYS
"SHOPPING."

Here I don't want it anymore.

HE TAKES THE NAME OUT OF HIS MOUTH
AND BLOWS IT BACK TO HER.

Here's your receipt. Excuse me, I have to get some change.

SHE LEAVES.

I love shopping.

George Whatever Bush, or It's in the Bagh, Dad

AMERICAN ECONOMY
Hi, I'm the American economy.
I'm getting shittier and shittier.
I think I'll join the army.... Oh, nooo....
I'm putting down the soldiers. I can't do this play.
It's very good and funny, but it'll ruin my career!
Like what happened with the,
    the, you know, Hot Chicks? Uh—

AMERICAN ECONOMY LEAVES.
ELECTIONS AND DEATH-WISH ENTER.

ELECTIONS
Hi, I'm a friend of Bill Clinton. They call me "Elections."

DEATH-WISH
You'd be good in Iraq, man.

ELECTIONS
What if they elect a Shiite Muslim
who reveres the Ayatollah Khomeini?

DEATH-WISH
Yeah, you know, I mean
    elections you can fix,
  like what the founding fathers wanted.

ELECTIONS
I love it when you brief me.

DEATH-WISH
SU-PAIR!

ELECTIONS
Let's debate!!!

BOTH EXIT. RIGHT WING AND AMERICAN
ECONOMY ENTER FROM DIFFERENT WINGS.

RIGHT WING
Wow, the American economy in Iraq!

AMERICAN ECONOMY
Have we met?

RIGHT WING (LIKE "BOND. JAMES BOND.")
Wing. Right Wing. (HE SHAKES HER HAND WITH RIGHT ELBOW.)

AMERICAN ECONOMY
Nice to meet you. What are you doing for Lent?

RIGHT WING
Giving up taxes.

AMERICAN ECONOMY
It will be interesting to see if it works.

RIGHT WING
Yeah, it's been on my to-do list.

AMERICAN ECONOMY
Why not? (PUTS UP ARMS IN CUTE, CRUCIFIED POSE)

RIGHT WING
No Reason! I wing it. It's hard work
exerting maximum shit on the exact number of
people so there aren't enough
     to get a recount!

AMERICAN ECONOMY
WOW OOO EEE! You're the kind of guy a perky
economy can be seduced by. You're pure sex.
     ...I should be scared.

RIGHT WING
You're right. I'm not LIKE the sixties; I AM the sixties.

AMERICAN ECONOMY
I don't disagree with you!

THEIR GLANCES INTERLOCK.

RIGHT WING
Okay, I have a secret:
The war's never going to end!

WHY ARE WE IN IRAQ?

AMERICAN ECONOMY
What a relief! I love Tantric war!

RIGHT WING (LOOKING)
What a lovely daybreak. I LOVE Operation Iraqi Freedom.

AMERICAN ECONOMY
I hope it never ends! Have a great day
        number whatever here.

RIGHT WING
It's so peaceful in Iraq. (HIS CELL PHONE BEEPS.
HE READS SCREEN ON PHONE.)
Kuwait a second!!!! Good news!!!
        The U.S. Supreme Court
just ordered the Arabs to go reconstruct themselves!!!
The Court wouldn't do THAT
if they weren't going to call
the whole damn world for me!!!
I'll have to give Scalia's kids
Supreme Court seats forever
    but I want to anyway.

AMERICAN ECONOMY
I know. I overheard our president
say "It's in the bag, Dad" to one of his fathers.

RIGHT WING
Well, time to preserve the hard won peace.
We've hearts and minds to titillate. It's such torture.

AMERICAN ECONOMY (SHE KISSES HIM.)
Put me in your coalition of the unwilling.

THEY SIMULATE SEX

RIGHT WING
Oh yeah.

AMERICAN ECONOMY
War's not sexy, it's sex.

RIGHT WING
That will be 75 billion dollars.

AMERICAN ECONOMY (SWEETLY)
You're a murderer, but you're my murderer.

Could you dial my go-for-broker?
(HE PUNCHES HIS CELL PHONE
AND HANDS IT TO
HER.) Buy 75 billion dollars in bonds
from foreigners who hate our guts
and know what jerks we are to let
the right wing kill and maim forever.

RIGHT WING
Hey, it's only infinite justice.
I forget why now, but I need absolute
control and some uh money. Who could
know the terrorists would fight so dirty?
Terrorists used to be so nice! (PHONE
RINGS. RIGHT WING ANSWERS.)
Uh oh, the Chinese are dumping bonds.
You're in default, bitch.

IRAQ IRAN THE CLOCK

AMERICAN ECONOMY
WHAT AM I GOING TO DO!!! (PHONES SOMEONE)
Hello, Brazil, could you loan me three billion dollars for a
cup of coffee? (HANGS UP) (TO RIGHT WING AGAIN)
You said there was no downside to running up my debt!

RIGHT WING
There isn't. The International Monetary Fund and World
Bank want ME to help YOU put YOUR house in order.

AMERICAN ECONOMY
But I can't go home now. I'm still mopping Iraq.

RIGHT WING
Man, Clinton gave you some bad intelligence!

AMERICAN ECONOMY
Yeah, I could tell it was HIS intelligence. It tasted
funny. Not bad, but funny.

RIGHT WING
You could join the Moonies?

AMERICAN ECONOMY
So there's no problem. I think we've got an awful pretty day ahead. The
sand's already kicking up.

RIGHT WING
Yeah, what the hell, a-hard wind's gonna blow me.
The nation will rejoice. I got my PATRIOT missile....
      I got my PATRIOT act.

AMERICAN ECONOMY
And they're all so liberating.
We're not too young to love.
I wish these armchair genitals, I mean generals,
would stop second guessing our shock and bore lifestyle. It's not much, but
we like it.

RIGHT WING.
WE BOMB. YOU ENJOY.

Living with You Is a Community

I wish we could go downstairs and it would be Bombay.
Your concept of a concept is not my idea of sense.
I'd like us to remember ourselves and be summer.
"I've gone through all my mother's milk," says Jill
                            in a play that isn't by her.
Sugarless soda cuts sugar dead (which is a carrier of thirst).
"You'll have to go downstairs and get sugar if you
want coffee," says Bob in his West 48th Street apartment,
"but in this neighborhood you might get sugar-cane."
"Well, D.C. is in first place," Bob continues, "What do you
                                          think?"
And he shows me the banner headlines about beheading.
Pat says, "I'm going to Washington for the weekend ... to
                            have fun."
She doesn't know from the news,
the capitol running around like a chicken.

2.
"I close my eyes and I see
        Hawaii," and she says,
            "I see images like that—India."
He'll just be fucking for the rest
        of his life.
We read parts of "A Fragment"
        and fuck intermittently.
They go short distances with great success.
Another man waits a week for a Czech girl.
What did they wear in Japan? Ties.

3.
It ended in neutrality.
Spring's here and tastes
        like summer.
Bob and I walk into fall.
"There's a Baba-lover working there,
        but she's not upper-crust.
        I really go for that upper-
        crust illusion," says Bob.
Suddenly, I'm miserable.

4.
What do you say to a hijacker?
"I like the way you play your instrument?"
Or, Kenny suggests, "What do you call that thing?"
Doesn't New York make you a little sad
the way a gun is useless when it's art
or a whistle given to every citizen over
        65 to stop crime?
It's so expensive to marry for money,
you give up such a homelessness.

5.
These are small poems, that's what they are.
We're on the wrong side of the museum.
We have to walk a U-turn down Fifth Avenue, O Boy!
Last time Bob walked down Fifth Avenue he
        met Jill!

6.
Some people have been hot for years. Look
at these guys. They are always writing
our poetry. I remember eating a hot dog
in a woman's face during Christmas season
on Fifth Avenue. Constantly I run into
people I know. They tear me apart but I
make it up in tears. "Once I was walking
up Fifth Avenue and a girl followed me,"
        says Bob.

7.
"She was heavily following
        me," Bob continues.
We unbutton our jackets
on Fifth Avenue and gush.
A girl with very long red hair
        tries to pick Bob up. He does
        not care.

8.
"I don't know your name,"
says a Jumbo 747 to a Dutch girl,
nothing left of them but the accident.

9.
We can only discuss essence in pairs.
"I might be Willy Brandt" is one discussion of essence,
     but obviously there are two of us.

10.
I don't gain any weight in traction.
I just lie there in silent talent.
My nurse tells me about letters.
"There's nothing in this envelope."
     she gulps at the tongue
  inside another one as the day
melts into another
     reason to enjoy it.

11.
Any lie you
tell will be
the truth, unless
it takes into
account imperfection like
the freckles on
a gallery's face
or a small
cigarette close-up
dried-out matches
the color of dust,
the orange price-tag.
Did you notice
the city? So
he washed his
spectacles. It was
seafood in the
form of an
object before him,
No, really It
was love in
the form of
a girl for
him.

10.
I edit before I write from decisions I never
     think of.

I feel I must be me in the absence of myself
but cream at the thought of someone else being it,
                          or doing it?
I ask you to decide and these decisions crush me.
I'd rather you present me with a palette of pies
    than throw one in my face.
What was the pie, blueberry? "You don't have peach?
                            But fuck peach."
A talented man could tell a critic about fruit.
A critic might make an art of eccentric ideas
    about fruit.
But the bulbs of art are not fruit. Pooh
puts a knife through art about art.
I make a pie of it
which if a fruit could be eaten.
Art about art is a lush merry-go-round
blown through a straw. We are all awakening
on our constructs of raw space emotion.
Two "w"'s around an "o" make "wow."
We point to ourselves in the mirror of you.
Emotion into emotion makes empathy. We both
are what we feel. It makes us look dumpy
to wear hats that make us look better than we
feel. Others of us are caught between
necessity and necessity, making a mess.

You take all your points of view
and make a juice. Stephen Paul Miller likes this.

Iraq Iran the Clock

B-Morning, I'm George Whatever Bush.

WILD APPLAUSE. REPUBLICAN LEADERSHIP GOES ONSTAGE.

R-Christ. Jesus Christ. A.K.A. Republican Leadership.

B-Oh yeah, aren't we supposed to talk, I mean, about something?

R-The assault gun ban?

B-Wanna extend it?

R-I sure want to. D' you?

B-I'll do whatever you want.

R-Do you want to extend it?

B-Only if you do.

R-But I want what you want, of course.

B-Don't be afraid to tell me your feelings.

R-You won't laugh at me?

B-No, I always like a nice extension.

R-Well, good luck with it.

B-You need luck?

R-No, I mean NO I SURE DON'T.

B-Believing is seeing. It's easy to be decisive when you're completely out of touch. Forget problems, there're only final solutions.

R-Fudge! We missed the assault gun ban
                        extension deadline.

B-It's not your fault!

R-But I loved that ban!

B-Pretend nothing ever happened.

R-I'll try.

You Think Your Dream Is Real Because You Can't Feel the Bed

35 plays by Noah and Stephen Miller

When you
    take
        my dignity,
            I get mad.

      When did you realize that?

                I heard it on *SpongeBob*.

   * * *

Where is that tall glass building?

    Long Island City,
       but Long Island City
          is really in Queens.

              Figures.

   * * *

If soda and juice evaporate,
why doesn't it rain soda and juice?

   * * *

There are more kids than adults.
New kids are born everyday.

    But kids become adults
        everyday.

But they have more kids,
and it takes a long time
for an adult to be born.

   * * *

We might go to war in Iraq.

Oh my God! All the world is a rock!!!

   * * *

Don't blame me. I voted for George Washington.

   * * *

Why are more people in Manhattan than Staten Island?

    Maybe Manhattan is nearer other places,
    or maybe Manhattan is flatter,
    or maybe people came to Manhattan first.

I think people came to Manhattan first.
Adam and Eve lived in Manhattan.

    * * *

I didn't want to take a chance
and talk with that stranger
who told me my yo-yo was cute.

    * * *

When you go broke,
    you can become mentally ill,
        and when you become mentally ill
            you can go crazy.

    * * *

Do doctors' doctors go to doctors?
        Is it a big circle?

    * * *

Do you remember when you said
    "if an elephant can camouflage
    then a camel can elephantage."

        Yes.

            Well, it's not funny anymore.

    * * *

If you eat another of my M&M's
I'll cut you open to get it back.

Don't be so violent.

I'm not being violent.
I'd put you back together.

    * * *

If life were rated, it would be X.

    * * *

*Well, there is a book with its author's name
named* Roland Barthes *by Roland Barthes.*

Rolling farts by rolling farts by rolling farts by
rolling farts by rolling farts by rolling farts.

    * * *

Its round shape tells you
    Union Square Park's
        the center of town.

    * * *

The baseball field looks
    like a fan,
        but not just any fan,
            a Chinese fan.

    * * *

Is matzo sacred?

    I guess so.

Then why did you eat it?

    * * *

Coney Island is a theme park without a theme.

    * * *

The rules of baseball
    should be changed
        so pitchers can score.
            Pitchers should get a point
                when the other team gets no points
                    so it would not be zero-zero in the 12th inning.

    * * *

There are no bad or good teams.
It just matters what ball
        park they're in.

    * * *

Once things start, they can never end. Too bad!
    I wish once things ended
        they could never start.
            Then we wouldn't have this stinking war.
                There'd only be the first war.

    * * *

A. J., do you ever wonder what the future will be like?
    No, A. J., not like that electric scooter—
not the past future—the present future!

    * * *

I'm sad elephants stand for Republicans.

    Most Elephants are really Democrats.

    * * *

Why are there so many American flags out now?
What's so great about America?

    In America you can say anything.

You can't say you don't like America.

> *Yes, you can.*

You can't say it in school.

> *Yes, you can.*

But you have to say polite things in school,
> and saying you don't like America
>> wouldn't be polite.

> * * *

I believe in the tooth fairy, Easter Bunny, and Santa Claus
> because their jobs happen.
>> Even if Aunt Millie
>>> is the Easter Bunny,
>>>> there's still an Easter Bunny.

> * * *

One president was so fat
twenty-three people could fit in his bath tub,
> and they needed strings
>> to put the president in.

> * * *

Is Camelot a real place?
Is it lost?

> *Yes.*

Do people live there?

> *Maybe, but they don't know it.*

Oh, I think they know it!

> *Then why is it lost?*
> *Why can't they tell people*
> *where they are?*

They can't get out.
Camelot is so lost
they're too lost
to go anywhere.

> * * *

> *Shoot!*

Daddy!

> *"Shoot" isn't a bad word.*

· 47 ·

In my world it is.

   * * *

  Let's see what The Today Show
  says about the war.

How can you see what they say?

   * * *

What if Iraq wins the war as soon as it starts?

  Nothing. We'll go home.

So the war is about nothing?

   * * *

If time moved at the speed of light,
  there'd be no time to go to school,
    no time to live.
  We'd live in all time.

   * * *

  I like airplane bathrooms
better than regular bathrooms.
I like sleeping in tents.
In a large space you have to get things, but in a small
   one you say "I'm here."

   * * *

God gave Noah a rainbow
to show his promise would
  always be broken.

   * * *

Life is a painting.

 Why?

  Because everything has color.
   If things didn't have color
    they'd be drawings, but life is a painting.

   * * *

You think every dream is real
because you can't feel the bed.

3. Overflowing Pockets

Officer Stephen Paul Miller

based on a police report

It is about 11 P.M. on November 11 1984.
I am working out of the 33rd precinct in Elmhurst.
My partner and I receive a radio communication
stating there is a three car collision
and one of the drivers is possibly intoxicated.

When we arrive at the scene, two of the drivers approach
                                                           us,
while one of the drivers stays in his 1985 Lincoln
                                             Continental.
The two other drivers say the driver of the Lincoln is
                     completely uncooperative
                                        and intoxicated.
When my partner asks the driver for his license,
                           registration, and
                                insurance card,
          the driver states, "Fuck you."
My partner then asks the driver to get out of the car
and again the driver states, "Fuck you."

My partner now realizes the driver is intoxicated,
reaches into the car and attempts to help the driver out
but is met with a sidekick aimed at his groin.
                                      It just misses.
I pull the still unidentified driver out
                        of the brand new Lincoln and,
when the driver attempts to hit me,
I block his punch,
countering his head butt with a right cross,
knocking the driver to the ground,
where he is cuffed and arrested
for driving while intoxicated and resisting arrest.
As soon as the driver is put into the marked police car
                           and read his rights,
he states to me, "You don't know who I am.
I'm John Gotti and I'm going to kill your mother.
Then I'm going to kill you. First I'm going to rape you.
Then I'm going to kill you slowly and then they'll find you
stuffed in a trunk in New Jersey. I did hard time for
                                         murder,"

he continues, "and this is shit. I've been sleeping in jail
                              with niggers all my life."

                         We proceed to
the precinct where an ambulance
           is dispatched for Mr. Gotti,
even though he does not request medical aid
                              nor want to go to the hospital.
When we all arrive at the 33rd precinct station house,
Mr. Gotti, who has blood on his face,
is asked by the desk officer,
a lieutenant, who was just transferred
                    from the Internal Affairs Division,
  "How did you you get in this condition, Sir?"
"I slipped and fell," Mr. Gotti answers.
I interrupt and say, "He didn't slip. He resisted arrest
And necessary force was used to affect that arrest."
Gotti screams at me, "What did you tell him that for?!
           That's between me and you!"
He is searched in front of the desk officer
and I confirm he is John Gotti of Howard Beach, Queens.
His funds are two thousand and seven hundred dollars.
He laughs and says, "That's chump change.
 I drop more in a crap game than you make in a year."

At about this time, Gotti receives a phone
                         call from his lawyer.
Gotti tells him he is going to another precinct for a
               breathalyzer test. When we get to
                    the only facility in Northern Queens
       with an intoxicated driver testing unit,
Gotti's colleagues, three large men all staring at the
                                        situation,
             are waiting in a black limousine.
    John Gotti fails two tests,
gets a desk appearance ticket, and is released.

   One week later, at approximately five A.M.,
I receive a phone call at my home from an unidentified male caller who says,
"Mr. Miller—"
  "Yes," I reply.
  "Your mother's dead."
  "You're an asshole," I say and hang up.

Cybersqualor

A friendly priest at the St. John's University
                Technology and Teaching Workshop
gives me a *Village Voice* "Jews in Cyperspace" article
suggesting Jewishness is about
     everything but being a Jew
        and internet wandering
            makes us all Jewish.
On TV, now, a rabbi keynotes Reagan's
                Judeo-Christian funeral
           bash.
I've lots of police in my family
   and the cop report below
strikes me as particularly Jewish
      since it's not Jewish at all
and more easily thought of as Christian:

'Police respond to strange odor.
discover Apt with 60 cats, 20 dead cats, so
                much debris they can't enter apt
     filled with venom, bugs, lice, mice, mites,
cockroaches, accumulation of years of collecting
garbage piled so high you would have
     to kneel when walking to keep from hitting the ceiling.
       A man in his 50s is living in the apt. with his mother.
   He says she died and was cremated,
but no records indicate she has been removed.
Police Emergency Service do a body search
with body suits and oxygen tanks.
After 2 hrs they say it is impossible
to search this place with rakes.
All the shit must be moved out.
Detectives are notified there
is an 80-something woman missing from the apt.
There is no light or running water.
When you flash a light it looks like
a1000 flashing eyes looking at you.
I interview the son of the missing woman.
The son is read his Miranda/interrogation warnings.
After waving them, he makes the following statement:

   ——On March 16th my mother passed.
I did not know she was dead until March 18th.

I was drinking heavy and passed out. I know I called
the funeral home to pick her up
and stayed drunk ever since.
She was 84 yrs and could not move for 4 yrs.
The main problem was cats and
they were hers in the beginning.

Please give me till Friday
to remove the cats. You can move
                            the things then.
I can't really say what time
she died but it was getting dark out.
                    I called the funeral home and
somebody came to pick her up. I never called
     the police. My mother was sitting up.—

I'm a Jewish Sherlock
searching through faint and exotic squalor.

Marilyn, as an Actress in a Play, Starts It

MARILYN:

Well, it's like the Anthrax thing.
What does it have to do
with the victim's life, anyway?
A flower pot drops on your head
and you find out Marilyn Monroe
dropped it or a baby is born
and she turns out to be Marilyn
or she takes acting lessons and
becomes fair and luscious. It
probably was the last thing she wanted.
When she plays dumb it's the mirror image
of her getting out of the way and letting the acting happen.
This afternoon I watched the end of a *Leave it to Beaver*
where Beaver wins a medal for making the best poster.
He won because all the other kids
had help from their parents.

So Beaver was very proud and all.

Ward Cleaver, you know, Beaver's father,
says it is a great temptation—
and he uses that word—
to help his son, like how Meher Baba says
it is his greatest temptation to that date—
1952 or 3—to give
sight to a blind boy crying Baba's name in the dark,
but he says he's able to resist the miracle
for the same reason I suppose that Mohammed says
His manifestation will be amazing because
He won't do any miracles. And I think we've
all lost sight of how neat the Arab world
is in the ninth century A.D....or B.C.

When Beaver comes home
he is very happy in his dead pan
      way
and hands the medal to his father.

When his father asks what it's for,
                    Beaver says, "for doing nothing."
So that's how Ward Cleaver is a lot like Marilyn Monroe,
                    when you think about it.

Overflowing Pockets

1

"Hello, Stephen, this is someone you did'n—you never
expected to hear from again. Uh, it's Marcy Murray, I'm
Mark Murray's sister, and I met you in New York oh *years*
ago—maybe about four years ago,

and you sent me a tape of a really interesting performance,
and I enjoyed the tape and I really appreciated your sending
it to me, and I never sent it back to you, and I wanted to
confirm that I still had

your address and phone number, and to apologize for not
sending you the tape back. But, uh, I will get it back to you
now. If it's convenient I'm coming
to New York ah-um, in a week and I'll be there

for two weeks, and I can drop it off at your house if you're
in town or I can mail it to you—" My message machine
cuts Marcy off. I look through
boxes of old computer discs to see if I can find

the address file with her number. I think of calling
friends for her brother's number, but I figure I might more
easily find hers, and anyway,
as she tells me when I finally speak with her,

Mark doesn't have a phone. Without too much trouble,
I find her number (I suppose she doesn't leave another
message because she assumes I expect her to
call again next week when she's in New York).

I leave a message saying I'm happy to hear from her
and looking forward to having "coffee or something" in
about a week, at which time she
can give me the tape. That would be better than

mailing it to me, since I would then not need to go to the
Post Office. The next afternoon, the phone rings and my
hello

is met by Marcy's thoughtfully hesitant "Hello,
Stephen." She inflects on an uninflected base. For
instance, in her message, the kind of sing-
song quality emitted through her string of phrases

beginning with "and" nonetheless swings on such turns as
"and I wanted to confirm." I ask how she is and I
guess she says good, and
            then I ask if she can hold on a minute

(while I turn down WNYC—I don't turn it all the way
down since I think I might be able to follow the Grace
Paley story and LBJ discussion and still talk with her at the
            same time, but I can't). How are things in

Santa Monica? In telling how much easier it's than New
York, she eventually stresses the largeness of the
apartments. That's why you don't meet
            anyone on the streets or in any public context.

Socializing is done in the homes—not in restaurants or
coffee shops. In L.A., you meet new people at parties. You
have to be invited. (I compare
            the ferocity with which I just saw

the San Francisco Giants eliminate the Los Angeles
Dodgers from the pennant race with the Dodgers' apparent
"Who invited you?" attitude toward the
            Giants.) Marcy says that L.A. is changing a little.

There are more coffee shops now, and poetry readings
are a relatively new L.A. phenomenon that is
springing up in many neighborhoods—It sounded as if
            there are more surplus people around

now—people who do not fit evenly within a domestic
underground—and they've enough economic
clout to have their own poetry reading environment
            marketed to them. I tell Marcy I

never heard L.A. described so succinctly. She says she
"had twenty years to…" "—Crystallize it," I say.
I can't tell how satisfied she is with my word.

She says she much prefers San Francisco but her work
brings her to LA. Has she seen our mutual acquaintance? "
"No, I only saw Howard Levander once." "He's in Oregon now,"
            I tell her, "or at least he was in 1978—He's become a

real dude…. He was working as an electrician and he was a
completely different Howie. He couldn't believe that a
couple of friends of mine and I still seemed to be trying for
            the same kinds of things we

tried for as teenagers. You know what I mean?"
"Yes," she says understandingly. "After I saw you," I say,
"in 1986 or 7 or 8, I called up Oregonian information, but
there was no Levander listed in the state of Oregon. So, I

don't know, he might not be in Oregon now. I think I tried
Washington information too. He had become a real Great
Northwest Kingdom working class guy. I asked him if he
went to California much and he said,

'Neah, California is for faggos.'" Marcy seems confused
as to what to say. I just mean to point out
what Howie seems like at the time. "They hate

California in Oregon," Marcy explains. "I know, but I
mean the term struck me as a weird combination of Oregon
and Rego Park dialect.
I told the word to a gay New York poet named

Kenward Elmslie who immediately put it in an abstract
poem and published it," I add, perhaps to excuse myself.
"I only saw Howard once,"
repeats Marcy. "He lived in the same building

I did. Howard seemed different from most of the people
who lived there. It was a depressing part of my life."
"Yeah," I commiserate, "that was an eerie Queens high
rise. Alexander's seemed so

omnipresent." "That sign flashed on and off into my
bedroom," she says with a flat poignancy that confirms
my observation. I feel so sorry for
her. She tells me she stayed there

until 1972, then made her way to San Francisco, and then
eventually to L.A., primarily because she works in films. I
try to remember her exact line of film work. "I met
Howard outside my building.

He was reading William Blake. He read some poems to
me." She conveys how great Blake's poetry seems to
her in 1968 or 9.
They take a long walk.

I note that Howie reads Blake in large part because
I tell him how great he is. "I was a year older than him.
I was like an older brother. I'd get excited about something
and Howie would get

· 58 ·

excited about it. Do you remember how Howie would get
excited? That's why I remembered your first name almost
twenty years after Howie mentioned you to me. When
              your brother introduced you as Marcy

I immediately asked you if you knew Howie Levander
because, I don't know, there might be a lot of Marcys but
it just seemed natural that you were
   the one Howie was talking about. Howie only

mentioned you once to me—He just said that he met a
really great girl named Marcy in the same way that he
might say he just read a really great Blake poem.
     Howie's younger sister Wendy had a McCarthy poster

on the wall and I somehow saw your name in it. Every
time I saw Eugene McCarthy's name I saw your name in
it." I tell her
     I know it seems strange.

2

I read the first part of this poem to Marcy when we get
together in October. She says that she liked my read on her
speech pattern—that she does think things out as she
      speaks, that she was genuinely

surprised that the Howie she knew would use the word
"faggo" because he struck her as gay.
     She describes her tape editing work for

The Entertainment Cable Network. It seems very subtle,
but she says it isn't as rewarding as it used to be because
cost-cutting measures caused the network
      to present the product and soundtrack in advance.

· 59 ·

She'd like another editing job. She looks back fondly on
her work editing *The Gong Show*. She says her
brother Mark looks down on her
            for making a living on such commercial things.

I tell her I can't understand her brother—she can
use her job for her own ends, and, anyway, I'm envious of
the important cultural work she's doing.
    She tells me many more people see a low-rated
television show than blockbuster movie. Marcy is a
Buddhist, and she takes me to The Anthology Film
Archives, where she hasn't been before, to see a Tibetan
    Buddhist movie about a master's reincarnation as a child.

I get to stand next to Cindy Crawford and Richard Gere, and don't
recognize them for a few minutes as we all wait on line inside,
though I know Cindy is a model because she
            looks like one,

though I wasn't drawn to her, so I concentrate on Gere
because he's apparently the kind of guy who dates
models and from that prospective seems more
                    impressive

than Cindy. After the movie, Richard
rises suddenly from his seat to
tell everyone this was the best Tibetan
            Buddhist movie he's ever seen.

We speak to the film director who says that the key was
getting to know everyone he filmed. Afterwards, Marcy
and I eat at the Tibetan restaurant on Second Avenue,
    where Marcy tells me she is pregnant with her first child.

I can't help but bring up the possibility of a Tibetan
master in the wings. Marcy does in fact have a calming,
contemplative effect on me. Before flying back to
    California, she leaves a very
            cordial message
        on my machine.

4. Hustling

Skinny Eighth Avenue

That involuted rush of
        getting over your
        cold while its symptoms
        are stifled.
There's nothing in-between the programs
        and the errors we make
        in them.
We appreciate you on your
        purely stiff level but
        other friends see in you
        the mother.
This poem has a mind that's
        only half-full but calling
        attention to itself it
        slushes.
Now every hour is occupied
        or to say my day is
        air-tight or only
        a vacuum by which
        metabolism can leap-frog.
I think I've sort of got it,
        I've fallen into the thickets,
        feel the strawberries crown
        my efforts.
Let's just say there is something
        beyond relationships, an
        invisible fudge where
        you'd expect to find butter,
        gumming up all the oars
        as we try to row out of it.
I've missed a chance to say
        something. I haven't rowed a boat
        for ages, no wonder
        it reminds me of
        churning butter;
But it's too late to call forth a comment
        you understand already. I know you know
        all things must have something
        to be relative to if they are to be relative
        and in this intangible sense something
        or other is absolute, the superficial
        layers gathered by the hillside.

It could be a blender too,
        I love the way they grind
        Italian Ice and
        get it so soft.
That exhausts texture, what
        I want to talk about now,
        since I somehow feel
        that you are the invisible
        fudge, that I could
        not talk unless you were
        listening, that you are
        the absolute who interrupts
        my inert collection of
        time-spans, that whether
        I can see you or not
        is another question, that I
        constantly need a reminder
        of how much I need you, is
        how much better cherry
        is than lemon or pineapple,
        I guess because an idea
        behind its sucrose, its
        flavor, overwhelms its
        synthetic constituents
      with the help of its texture.

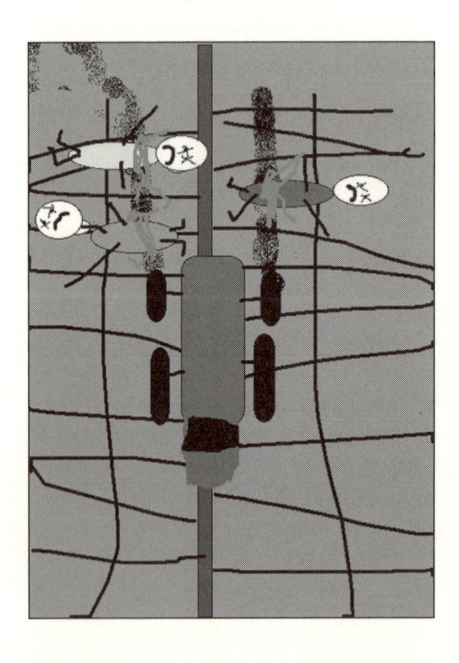

"The Hustle" and Its Liquid Totems
of Holocaust, Suburb, and Computer

We believe in unverifiable
Republican-owned-and-run Diebold machines
and the mere coincidence
of exit polls being
well within margins of error
in precincts not
using such machines
while Bush enjoys five percent bumps over exit polls
where Diebolds are used,
demonstrating faith in the hustle.
Hey, ya gotta believe.

If we really voted
for senseless war and
the world of woe
offering the poor
no option but to fight them
then "The Hustle" is
the latest dance
and you really have to do it.
Claude Lévi-Strauss speaks of totems
as tools of thought.
The Dinkas think trucks
 and typewriters
  the totems
   of the Westerners studying them,
    notes Lévi-Strauss,
     poking holes in a misconception that
      totems are either plants or animals
       and suggesting totems can be anything
        organizing conscious and unconscious cultural
                                        production.

                         Assuming
                          we experience
                          a major
                          cultural
                          shift
                          after
                          World War II,

· 65 ·

what are our
post-WWII totems?
I think there are three
monster
phenomena the three totems
are based on:
(1) holocaust(s)
co-opting
notions of progress away
from Enlightenment thought,
(2) the computer
antithesisizing the Holocaust
in that the computer is rooted
in Enlightenment desires
by Leibniz and others
for a universal solution
to all problems, and the
computer has a
causal relation with the
Holocaust in that Alan Turing
invents it to break the German
Enigma
code to sink unwitting U-boats
and thus let needed American
supplies
reach England,
although his 1935 theoretical
brainstorm eventually enabling
the computer
is a by-product of proving logical
and mathematical operations
don't all relate
or refer
to any numerical reality
and hence Turing like the Nazis revises
Enlightenment mind-sets but in a way prefiguring both
sixties cultural radicals and mainstream liberals—Related
to this, I think,
the totem of Holocaust and holocausts
is one unconscious way to organize
huge national populations
when correspondingly
Americans need to think
of the United States

                    as a tangible, verifiable New Deal-related
community (concerning liberals
compare "freedom through work" and "benign neglect,"
and note the ambivalence
of post-World War desires to integrate
contrasted with de facto inner city segregation,
and concerning the radical left,
note Nazism as an emblem
of what so-called hippies don't want) and
                    (3) the suburb,
                the dominance
            of it after all perhaps the major
            World War II outcome—
            and I'm not referring to what suburbs
            have become or may become—
            but rather I mean the classic post-World War II
            suburb as a synthesis of the Holocaust and the computer—
            creating on the one hand a Holocaust-related
            majoritive whitey-o-world
            and on the other an ongoing,
            rational, easily marketable, nature as commodity,
            Enlightenment world.
        You can organize the totems differently.
        I take nuclear holocaust,
            television,
        and the Cold War
        as secondary totems
        metaphorically,
        in terms of their places
        in our collective unconsciousnesses,
        made of what, arguably,
    are what I consider the primary three totems:
    Holocaust(s), computer, suburb.
    Note totems aren't phenomena.
    Turing's work goes on
to lay a groundwork for Emergence, Chaos, Complexity,
and String Theories,
    but I'd relate these to the computer totem.
    How do you use these totems if at all?
        Are all cultural phenomena made of these three totems?
        Maybe.
            Take "The Hustle":
            Dah dah, dah dah,
                dah ta

      dah dah ta ta dah dah,
     da tah
     do it
        do the hustle!
woo woo woo
    do the hustle!
     Well, disco itself,
      and I know Van McCoy,
       who wrote "The Hustle,"
     might be oblivious
      to disco, is significant
     for being a minority,
    a gay and a black,
      appropriation of majority white
     straight
      appropriations of black music.
       It seems to me "The Hustle"
        is critical in this counter-appropriation
       because it takes a light
      foreground as a background
       suburban construction
        of muzak—perhaps black musicians
       playing muzak figure out how
        to use it for themselves. This smooth
       relatively featureless quality
        reminds me of the suburban-related
       hula-hoop (a "hula-caust"?).
       I know that Van McCoy
       says he knew
       nothing of the dance,
      "The Hustle,"
      but still as a cultural
       construction, the dance
       dynamically ironizes
        white, country line-dance.
       Before "The Hustle,"
        previous disco music
         albeit some of it also written
by Van McCoy such as "Don't Rock the Boat"—no
relation to U-Boats—or is there?—
                        is light
                         rhythm and blues.
                        I might be wrong
                        and welcome

correction, but
it seems to me
"The Hustle" brings
dance down.
Eventually, disco
makes the buttocks
a virtual limb
by highlighting
hand and foot
moves and
centers on butt
propulsion,
though vertical
emphases

underscore

horizontal
suburban
space. The
computer-
totem
factors in
with the
image
of the
hustle
itself.
A work
of genius
like
McCoy's
song
works
smoothly
through
many ad hoc
musical
operations
as does
Turing's insight
of the computer

itself.

McCoy's
complexity
accommodates

................................and massages our
................................underlying urges
simply
....to do it like either the final
solution for a Nazi or Universal Love in the sixties
and the Hustle as a dance is not the same as being conned
by Reagan and George W. Bush-totems, which I contend
................................can run an ethical
................................spectrum—before
................................Nike's (in this Greek goddess regard
note
................................the 1936 Berlin
................................Olympics do much
................................to innovate
................................seeming Greek traditions
................................such as portable
................................Olympic flames)
................................campaign there are
................................adaptations of a Nazi call
................................to jettison inhibitions on
................................our natural inhibitions.
................................How politically correct
................................could Hitler have been?
................................I imagine "Do it"
................................is long standing sexual
................................performance slang
................................but as political concept
................................I associate it with a
................................sixties break
................................from notions of the possible.
................................In this regard, I posit
................................the sixties as a better version
................................of Holocaust nature/people
................................unifications. Let's hustle
................................as we come to terms with what
................................Holocaust, computer, and suburb
................................totems are—liquid totems—totems
................................structuring cultural ambivalences after
................................World War II that are "liquid"
................................in that they constantly
................................reconfigure themselves,
................................often in relation one to another.
................................Culture is the stuff liquid totems
................................freeze into.

        A totem isn't history
          or a historical phenomenon.
        The totems of the Holocaust,
      computerizations, and suburbanization
      are not the same as their respective historical
      events (or sets of events or phenomena) even if
     phenomena and totems interrelate. I
    characterize the Holocaust totem
   as something like categorical
  entitlement
or dehumanization and/or annihilation
            and/or disenfranchisement.
        Computer totems involve
      a merging of functionality and emergence,
      that is, the shaping of a whole through its smallest
      parts and/or models. The suburbanization totem
      concerns divisions of work and home and privilegings
      of private and public spaces. "The Hustle" reverses
     the post-World War II era totemic order, starting
    with a suburban synthesis being undone. McCoy,
   is in this period experimenting with various
   branches of international third-world music and the exotic
  woo---woo-woo-woo harmonies evoke a suburban
 kind of nature-commodification building to
 categorical release, a positive holocaust light, mass
 individualized light and life and infinitely verifiable reason
   that is co-opted by the play of full grooved operations
     in McCoy's fluty hustle. Love, Stephen Paul Miller. See You soon.

· 71 ·

5. Photo Posts

Photo Post

The white of your shorts pocket lining
matches the little Frosted Flakes bag.
You are nothing but birth suspicious
the grounds of your birth have been
lifted, you stay at the corner
of the picture and
away from me,
connected to a thread.

All Visual Materials Emit Countless Cartoon Bubbles

for Mario Mezzacappa

I don't know about this poem
    I can't be there for it—
       I mean literally—
I have a personal commitment
and can't attend
the Taking Art to Heart's
art exhibition's
    opening/poetry reading
for which this poem is being written
     so as to be "inspired"
  by Jacqueline Goossens's photograph
           entitled "Nowhere to Go."

I really like the color Xerox
they gave me of the photo.

A number of poets were asked
 to be inspired by artworks of their choice
(they're really reproductions of artworks
placed on a table in a new art gallery
on Bay Street in Staten Island).
This information
may be particularly useful to

readers
who are not at the art show,
know nothing of it,
do not see or read this poem
   hanging on the gallery wall,
and may
be unfamiliar with Goossens's photo.
Those who encounter
         this poem
next to that photograph
on the wall of the Taking Art to
               Heart Gallery
during their benefit exhibition
   to aid the homeless on Staten Island
form one circle within the quantitatively
larger circle of billions upon billions

of potential readers. But then again
those at the art show
     might be this poem's only audience

but that's okay. That audience after all
"takes art to heart" and
therefore is committed
 to Staten Island's fuller, more

magnanimous articulation.
And yet, whichever audience
                              you're a part of,
the photograph here is there—is pushed
                    in and out of your view—
between the two kinds of audiences—here
                              and there—
and I'm not even here—in the happening,
promised land
              audience—
I'm at some all day workshop in
                        Manhattan and,
you see, for me Staten Island takes
              on a comfortable, weird
                              biblical taint—
it's where I spent my childhood,
and now I commute to it every day
on the ship in this photograph.
Well, not really, but I am
getting used to the new ferries,
and today I'm getting a ride across the
bridge—the bridges really—
the Brooklyn and the Verrazano....
In a way this process is like
bridges...or maybe Dixie Cups.
I mean you go from the photo to the poem
but you also go back again.
Loosely speaking, there's communication,
and then again there's also translation,
which I think comes from the Latin
for moving a dead priest's body.
I'm translating the photo
for better or worse.
Okay, I admit it, I'm afraid of the photo,

but I'm also clearing a space for it,
and I'll speak to it
in a little while—translate it that way—
whether or not anyone wants a translation,
I mean a semiotic
          equivalence—obviously
              I can't speak for it.

Can this poem be
   a kind of cartoon bubble?
Well, I suppose it can
in the context of knowing
        all
visual materials emit countless cartoon
       bubbles.
It seems so momentous to confront
     "Nowhere to Go."
What a coincidence Taking Art to Heart
asked me to write an ekphrastic
   poem—this poem—
an ekphrastic poem is a poem
    about a work of art,
since I'm writing a conference
   paper about ekphrasis.

Ekphrasis sheds light on
how poems work. Poems
   don't use images,
but rather set up worlds
between the two audiences of
meaning and the holding back of it.
Every writer is the object
   of her or his ekphrasis.
It's interesting that I'm not here now.
I'm going to ask Mario Mezzacappa,
a fine poet who attends my
creative writing workshop
at St. John's University on Staten
  Island if he can recite this for me.
That would be cool.
It would be part of the soup of this poem.
Ekphrasis is just the
   construction of subject matter—
whether the subject matter is present or not.

It's the Dixie Cups embedded
    in all our phrases
because the visual is the string
between the two speakers holding them.
It's our way, our linguistic way,
of seeing one another whether or

not we manifest that in an image.
James Heffernan, in *New Literary History*,
says that ekphrasis is the
  "verbal representation

of graphic
．　　　　representation."
That's true but you have to remember
visual representation happens
against a background
．　　　　　　of verbal representation,
and verbal representation occurs
．　against a background of visual
．　　　　　　representation.
Heffernan says ekphrasis creates
．　　　　a verbal mirror of the visual,
and yet those mirrors are
．　　　　　　present everywhere.
A picture comes replete with its own
．　　　　　　ekphrasis.
I am manifesting one ekphrastic
．　　　version of "Nowhere to Go,"
which is the unconscious of this poem,
as this poem is the unconscious of
．　　　"Nowhere to Go."
I was born on Staten Island and go
．　　　　　back everyday.
If you cross the bay one way, and you
．　cross the bay
the other way, you haven't crossed
the bay at all.
This pictures my life on the bay
writing this poem on the ferry
though it's really of a fifties
．　technicolor red streaked wooden boat
．　　　　　　hull.
I love the corroding orange red of
．　　　　　the hull's bottom.
Obviously this boat has
．　　　　　"nowhere to go"
but above that is the flying horse
．　　of the old I think Mobile logo.
(Did those signs have anything
．　　　　to do with Onassis?)
That winged horse, mediated by
the stone construction
atop I think a fenced-off canal,
is obviously going somewhere.
I like its flat appearance in
juxtaposition to
the three-dimensional

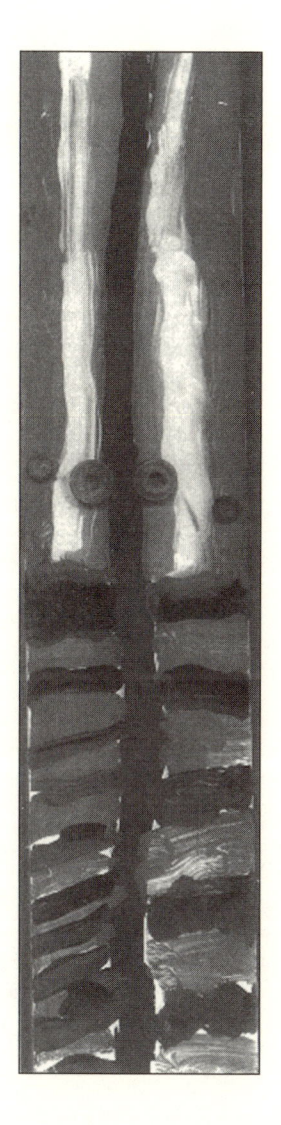

canal it seems to have kicked open.
He is of course Pegasus
who kicked a hole in Mount Helicon
                       releasing poetry.
There's a late not well known
Marx Brothers film
    that I saw on television
    when I was maybe three
    and have not seen since
    in which Harpo
    flies on the—is it the Mobile logo,
Pegasus?— through space—
   I think it was over a European city,
or maybe it was Casablanca.
Harpo, who is the very incarnation
             of non-verbal ekphrasis,
surveys the verbal kind
      from his ecstatic heights.
Words lap onto an island in
             the Aegean Sea
onto the boat in the photographic image
 of Jacqueline Goossens's photo.
From atop Pegasus, Harpo rises in midair.

This sad beauty is everywhere
     present in the photograph
    and I actively
      surrender
my life to it—
     the boat at the end
     of its identity
    but happy
    at the center of all tragedy,
      the upside down
     boat to the left
  punctuating it
  like a lid—holding
    the context in like bath water.
Where is the self-esteem in this,
    except in the image
     of the riderless
       Pegasus,
  and the Harpo it implies?

   After Mario dies a year later
I continue this poem for him,
        the riderless writer.

6. Devils' Wax

George W. Burning Bush

with Thomas Fink

    The new chief executive
        takes his oath with ease.
The White
       House chef powders up a lethal beverage
and the chief sips with patrician grace.
    A sunrise effect takes over.
     The tavern keeper changes channels.
Nixon knows people were happier before he was president,
                                                but he lives.

Devils' Wax

Let me hold this day up to a lightning bug
and throw an ash can through the glow.
The mountain peels off the monitor and
I expect to hear a whistle. Nothing blows but
Wallace Stevens's head breaks the stars
within one of St. John's University's fabulous game rooms.
Time falls on the surface and
chromosomes soar with
      party favors through Wally's open window.

Potato Chip

"Potato Chip lived a long life.
Remember the good parts,"
I tell Noah after his pet betta fish dies.
"There were no good parts," Noah cries.
"He was boring but I loved him."

ACKNOWLEDGEMENTS

Anita Feldman, Ilana Abramowitz, Sylvester Pollet, Jane Augustine, Angela Pontoriero, Dominick A. Casazza, Kenneth Deifik, S. Miller, Eric Miller, Taylor Mead, Billy Bergman, and others have read, edited, and added to parts of this book.

The author gratefully acknowledges the editors of the following magazines, in whose pages some of these poems have appeared: *Appearances, Backwoods Broadsides, Controlled Burn, Long Shot, National Poetry Magazine of the Lower East Side, New Journal, New Observations, Poetry New York, Poetry in Performance, Proteus, St. Mark's Poetry Project Newsletter, Sidereality, Talisman, Tamirand,* and *Telephone*.

Some of the poems were dramatically performed or academically presented at The Bowery Poetry Club, Center for Jewish History, Mid-Atlantic Popular Culture Association, St. Mark's Poetry Project, and 8BC.

St. John's University research grants and a sabbatical have helped make this work possible.

The University Seminars at Columbia University assisted in the preparation of this manuscript for publication. The ideas presented have benefited from discussion in the University Seminar on American Studies.

ABOUT THE AUTHOR

Stephen Paul Miller is a Professor of English at St, John's University in New York City. He is the author of *The Seventies Now: Culture as Surveillance* (Duke University Press, 1999). Miller is also the author of two books of poems, *The Bee Flies in May* (Marsh Hawk Press, 2002) and *Art Is Boring for the Same Reason We Stayed in Vietnam* (Domestic Press, 1992). He also, with Terence Diggory, co-edited *The Scene of My Selves: New Work on New York School Poets* (the University of Maine in Orono's National Poetry Foundation, 2001). Miller's work has appeared in *Best American Poetry 1994, boundary 2, Talisman, St. Mark's Poetry Project Newsletter, Backwoods Broadside, Sidereality, Sagetrieb, Long Shot, Another Chicago Magazine, Open City, Shofar, New Observations, American Letters & Commentary, The Wallace Stevens Journal, Boog City, Poetry New York, Columbia Review, Poetry New York, Mudfish, Le Petite Zine, Bowery Poetry Club website, Scripsi, Proteus, Tamarind, Appearances, The New Journal, Poetry in Performance, Paterson Review, Controlled Burn*, and elsewhere.

ABOUT THE ILLUSTRATOR

Noah Mavael Miller attends Frances Schuchman's third grade class at P.S. 41 in Greenwich Village, New York where he studies "Expression Art" with Phil Demise Smith. He has also studied art at the Guggenheim Museum, School of Visual Arts, and Children's Aid. His art and poetry won the PS 41/WQXR calendar competition in 2003 and 2004. The Drawing Center and the Bowery Poetry Club in New York City have exhibited his artwork. His poems were performed on WKCR in New York and published in *The National Poetry Magazine of the Lower East Side*. Noah says, "I'm interested in science, art, math, architecture, and design. So far I have made two films. I had seven fish in my entire life, and I will probably have more. I have three hermit crabs now, and like the fish, I will probably have more."

OTHER BOOKS FROM MARSH HAWK PRESS

GOSSIP, Thomas Fink
ARBOR VITAE, Jane Augustine
BETWEEN EARTH AND SKY, Sandy McIntosh
THE POND AT CAPE MAY POINT, Fred Caruso and Burt Kimmelman
THE BEE FLIES IN MAY, Stephen Paul Miller
MAHREM: THINGS MEN SHOULD DO FOR MEN, Edward Foster
REPRODUCTIONS OF THE EMPTY FLAGPOLE, Eileen R. Tabios
DRAWING ON THE WALL, Harriet Zinnes
SERIOUS PINK, Sharon Dolin
BIRDS OF SORROW AND JOY: NEW AND SELECTED POEMS, 1970–2000, Madeline Tiger
ORIGINAL GREEN, Patricia Carlin
SHARP GOLDEN THORN, Chard deNiord
HOUSE AND HOME, Rochelle Ratner
MIRAGE, Basil King
NATURAL DEFENSES, Susan Terris
BRYCE PASSAGE, Daniel Morris
ONE THOUSAND YEARS, Corinne Robins
IMPERFECT FIT, Martha King
AFTER TAXES, Thomas Fink
NIGHT LIGHTS, Jane Augustine
SOMEHOW, Burt Kimmelman
WATERMARK, Jacquelyn Pope

Marsh Hawk Press is a juried collective committed to publishing poetry, especially to poetry with an affinity to the visual arts.

Artistic Advisory Board: Robert Creeley, Toi Derricotte, Denise Duhamel, Marilyn Hacker, Allan Kornblum, Maria Mazzioti Gillan, Alicia Ostriker, David Shapiro, Nathaniel Tarn, Anne Waldman, and John Yau.

For more information, please go to http://www.marshhawkpress.org.